Albert Schweitzer
was a real person.
He lived from 1875 to 1965.
Schweitzer was a doctor,
a missionary, a musician,
a pastor, a writer,
and a teacher.
He loved all living things.
This is his story.

TABLE OF CONTENTS

The Schweitzer children in 1882. Left to right: Adele,
Albert, Margrit, and Louise.

Chapter 1

The Boy Who Thought

Young Albert Schweitzer
crept up the hill
behind the church.
He and his friend Henry
had made slingshots.
They were going to shoot birds.

Then the church bells
began to ring.
"You shall not kill,"
the bells seemed to say.
Albert jumped up.
"Shoo! Shoo!" he cried.
He would not let
those birds be killed.

I don't care what
the other boys think,
he told himself.
I think it is wrong
to hurt living things.

Later he learned that
some of the other boys
felt the same way.
They just hadn't been
brave enough to say so.

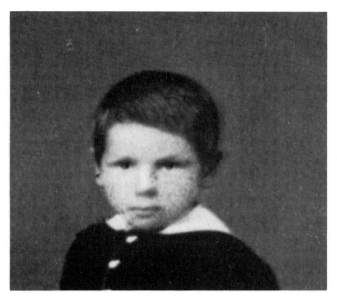

This is the earliest known
picture of Albert Schweitzer.
He is about five years old.

Albert grew up in
the town of Günsbach
in an area called Alsace.

Sometimes France owned Alsace.
Sometimes Germany did.
Albert learned to speak
both French and German.
He also spent a lot
of time thinking.

Left: Albert's mother, Adele Schillinger Schweitzer.
Right: Albert's father, Louis Schweitzer.

Albert's father was pastor
of a church in Günsbach.
He loved music.

Albert loved music, too.
He often thought about it.
And he learned to play
the piano and the organ.

But most of all, Albert
thought about nature
and living things.

Once he saw two men
pulling and beating
a tired old horse.
Albert never forgot that.

He wondered why people prayed
just for other people
and not for animals.

One night Albert made up
his own prayer.

"Heavenly Father,
protect and bless
all things that have breath,
and keep them from harm,
and let them sleep
in peace tonight."

That prayer made
Albert feel better.

Albert and his classmates at Günsbach school.
Albert is sixth from the left in the second row.

Chapter 2

Games and Work

Albert did not like school.
He wanted to be outdoors.

At first, he went
to school in Günsbach.
Then, when he was nine,
he went to school
in a town two miles away.

Albert liked the long walk
to and from school.
He spent the time
thinking about nature.

But when Albert was ten,
everything changed.
Now he had to go to school
in the city of Mulhouse.

Mulhouse was far from home.
So Albert had to live with
Uncle Louis and Aunt Sophie.

His aunt and uncle were strict.
Mulhouse was dark and gloomy.
Albert's schoolwork was hard.
Albert was not happy.

He did not do his schoolwork.
He daydreamed instead.
And he almost failed.

Albert liked his new teacher.

Then a new teacher
came to the school.
Albert liked him.
He helped Albert see
that hard subjects
were like games.

Albert decided to *win*
those games—and he did.
His grades got better
and he felt happier.
He made new friends
and he worked at his music.

Eight years later,
Albert left Mulhouse.
He went to the
University of Strasbourg.
Now Albert wanted
to learn all he could.

Albert studied religion
so he could be a pastor
like his father.
He studied philosophy—
different ways of thinking.
And he studied music.

These were good years.
Albert felt strong and happy.
But one thing worried him.
Shouldn't he be helping
people who were not
as lucky as he was?

Albert Schweitzer
as a young man,
about 21 years old

At last, when he was 21,
Albert made up his mind.
He would work at whatever
he wanted—
until he was 30.
Then he would spend
the rest of his life
helping other people.

**Schweitzer (front row, center) with his students
at the Theological College in Strasbourg**

Chapter 3

A New Life

The next nine years
flew by for Albert.

He became principal of
a college in Strasbourg.
He became pastor of
a little church there.
He played the organ
at another church.

This statue of an African deeply impressed Albert Schweitzer
when he was a young boy. He kept a plaster copy of the head
of this statue on his desk at Günsbach.

Albert wrote books, too—
books about religion,
philosophy, and music.

Then, when he was almost 30,
Albert read a little book
about people in Africa
who needed help.

Schweitzer at the University of Strasbourg, where he studied medicine

All at once, Albert knew
what he would do with
the rest of his life.
He would become a doctor
and help those people in Africa.

So Albert studied
to be a doctor.
It was not easy.
It took almost seven years.

Then Albert had to find
money to build and run
a little hospital in Africa.
He made speeches
and gave concerts.
His church helped.
His friends helped, too.

And so did Helene Bresslau.
She became a nurse so
she could work with Albert.
They got married in 1912.

Helene Bresslau
Schweitzer

Albert and Helene Schweitzer went to Africa to help people.

Above: Schweitzer on a hillside
near the Ogowe River.
Right: Today French Equatorial
Africa is called Gabon.

At last, in 1913,
the Schweitzers went to
French Equatorial Africa.
They went by boat
up the Ogowe River to
the town of Lambaréné.

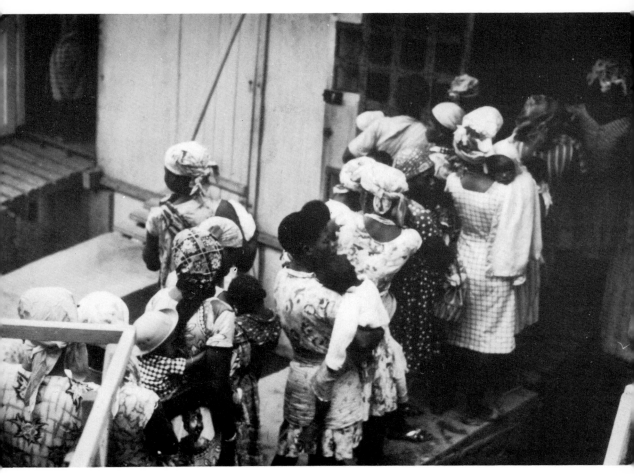

Africans came to Schweitzer for help in curing their diseases.

Albert hadn't even unpacked
when people began to come.
Some had diseases
from insect bites.
Some had been hurt by animals,
and some by other people.

Almost 2,000 people were treated in the first nine months at Schweitzer's first hospital. Many of the patients suffered from sleeping sickness.

At first, Albert helped them
outside his little house.
When it got too rainy,
he turned an old henhouse
into a hospital.

Albert wanted a real hospital
so much that he
helped build it himself.

Africans paddled their canoes to visit the hospital on the Ogowe River.

Then even more people came.
Some brought babies
who had no mother or father.
Some brought old people
who had no home.

"Let them come," said Albert.
"My hospital is open to all."

Parsifal, Dr. Schweitzer's pet pelican, used to follow him about.

Chapter 4

"Reverence for Life"

Albert helped thousands
of sick and hurt people.

He also helped animals—
baby antelopes, wild boar,
a little chimpanzee.
A pelican even made
its nest over Albert's door.

Dr. Schweitzer watching an operation at the Lambaréné hospital

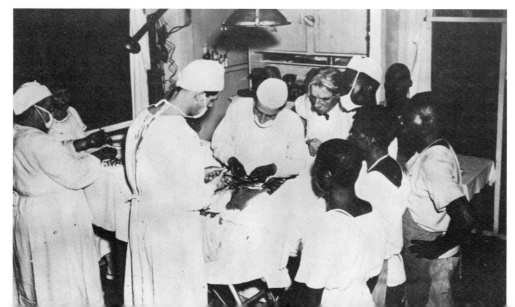

One day, Albert sat in
a boat on the river.
Nearby, hippos were
bathing and playing.
The setting sun made
a band of gold on the water.

All at once, three words
came into Albert's mind:
"reverence for life."

Those words meant that
all life was special.
Every living thing
wanted to live.
Every living thing
had a *right* to live.

Schweitzer and his cat Sizi. Schweitzer wrote about reverence for life. He hoped everyone would have respect for all living things.

What a good place the world
would be if everyone felt
reverence for life,
thought Albert.
He decided to write
a book about this idea.

Schweitzer as a prisoner of war in France. His native Alsace belonged to Germany during World War I, and he was considered an enemy by the French.

Then World War I began.
Albert and Helene
had to go back to Europe.
For a while they had to
live in a prison camp.

At last they got to Alsace.
But Albert's mother
had been killed by soldiers.

Albert broke down.
His body was sick,
His mind was tired.
It took him a long time
to get well again.

Why, oh why, couldn't people
feel reverence for life?

Schweitzer with his daughter, Rhena (right). Schweitzer in Alsace (below). Schweitzer spent part of his time in Europe after his daughter was born.

Chapter 5

A Man of Peace

After the war,
the Schweitzers stayed
in Europe for awhile.
They had a baby girl, Rhena.
Again, Albert worked
to make money for Africa.

In 1924, he was ready
to go back to Lambaréné.
From then on, he spent
part of his time in Africa
and part in Europe.

Lambaréné was not
a healthy place for
Rhena and Helene, though.
So sometimes Albert had to
go there without them.

Dr. Schweitzer with an African patient. His hospital
in Lambaréné had 300 beds for sick people.

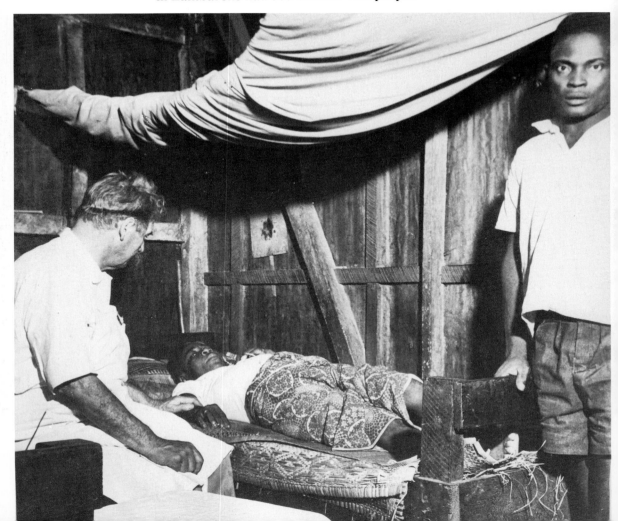

"Hospital street" at Lambaréné

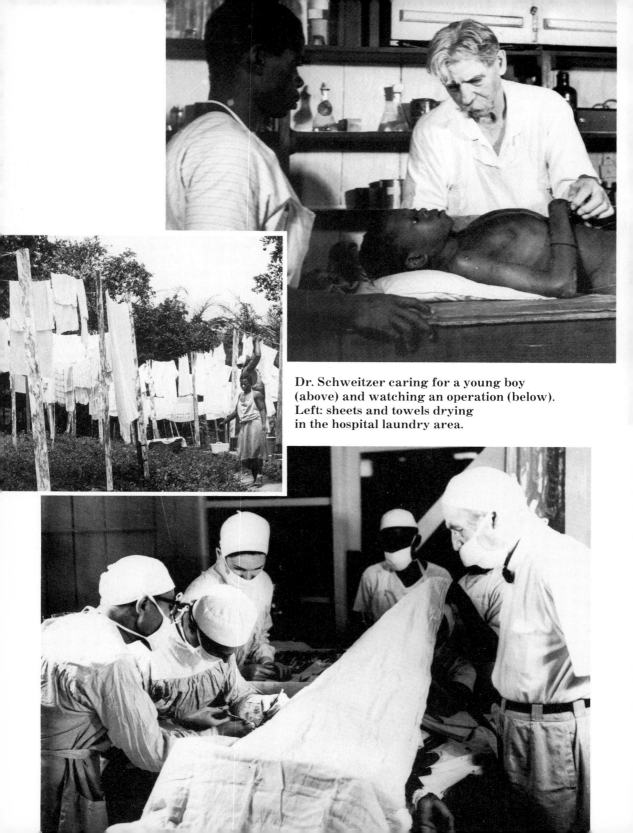

Dr. Schweitzer caring for a young boy
(above) and watching an operation (below).
Left: sheets and towels drying
in the hospital laundry area.

Patients and their families arrive at the Lambaréné hospital.

But Albert kept busy.
He built a new hospital
on high ground.
Around it, he grew food
for patients and workers.
As time went by,
more doctors and nurses
came to Lambaréné
to help Albert.

One evening in 1953,
a worker came to the room
where Albert was writing.

The worker had just heard
some news on his radio.
Albert had won the
Nobel Peace Prize for 1952.

When Albert heard that news,
he didn't say a word.
He just covered his face
with his hands.

Schweitzer (left) and his wife visited Oslo, Norway, in 1954.
Schweitzer gave a Nobel Prize lecture on the problems of peace.

Schweitzer helping children who have leprosy with
their lessons. They are writing on wooden tablets.

Schweitzer used his Nobel Prize money to
build houses for people with leprosy.

Albert also got money
with the prize.
He used it to build a village
for people with leprosy.
Now they could live in
good houses while they were treated.

41

The Schweitzers at
Lambaréné in 1957.
This was Mrs. Schweitzer's
last visit to Africa.

In 1957, Helene died.
From then on, Albert
stayed at Lambaréné.
But he wrote letters to
people all over the world.

Dr. Schweitzer writing letters at his desk in Lambaréné

In the letters,
Albert begged people
to work for peace.
Peace had to be part of
reverence for life.

Schweitzer had a special piano (above) made to resist the dampness of Africa's climate. The doctor holds one of his tiny patients at the hospital (right).

Dr. Schweitzer out for a walk with his beloved animals

Albert Schweitzer
died at Lambaréné
on September 4, 1965.
He was 90 years old.

He had loved all life
and he had made life better
for many, many living things.

Important Dates

1875   January 14—Born in Kaysersberg, Alsace, to Adele and Louis Schweitzer

1885   Began studies at Mulhouse

1893   Began studies at University of Strasbourg

1905   Began medical studies at Strasbourg

1912   Married Helene Bresslau

1913   Left for Lambaréné in French Equatorial Africa (now Gabon)

1919   Daughter Rhena born

1926   Built new hospital at Lambaréné

1953   Awarded 1952 Nobel Peace Prize

1965   September 4—Died at Lambaréné

INDEX

Page numbers in boldface type indicate illustrations.

PHOTO CREDITS

The Albert Schweitzer Center

The Albert Schweitzer Center is a museum, library, archive, wildlife sanctuary, and educational center in Great Barrington, Massachusetts. The Schweitzer Center's archives include films, photographs, manuscripts, and memorabilia of Schweitzer and filmmaker Erica Anderson. The center offers year-round educational programs, guided tours, and audiovisual presentations. The Wildlife Sanctuary, Children's Garden, and Philosopher's Walk are open all year during daylight hours.

Center hours are:

April 16—October 31	Tuesday through Saturday	10-4
	Sunday	11-4
November 1—April 15	Saturday and Sunday	11-4

ABOUT THE AUTHOR

Carol Greene has degrees in English literature and musicology. She has worked in international exchange programs, as an editor, and as a teacher of writing. She now lives in Webster Groves, Missouri, and writes full-time. She has published more than 100 books, including those in the Childrens Press Rookie Biographies series.